I Know That!

Smelling and Tasting

Claire Llewellyn

SEA-TO-SEA

Mankato Collingwood London

This edition first published in 2006 by
Sea-to-Sea Publications
1980 Lookout Drive
North Mankato
Minnesota 56003

Printed in China

Library of Congress Cataloging-in-Publication Data

Llewellyn, Claire.
  Smelling and tasting/by Claire Llewellyn
    p. cm. — (I know that!)
  Includes index.
  ISBN 1-932889-49-3
  1. Smell—Juvenile literature. 2. Taste-—Juvenile literature. I. Title.

QP458.L58 2005
612.8'6—dc22

                              2004062740

9 8 7 6 5 4 3 2

Published by arrangement with the Watts Publishing Group Ltd, London

Series advisers: Gill Matthews, nonfiction literacy consultant and Inset trainer. Editor: Rachel Cooke.
Series design: Peter Scoulding. Designer: James Marks. Photography: Ray Moller unless otherwise credited.
Acknowledgments: Chris George/Corbis: 21.Bryan Gibb/Art Directors/Trip: 7b. Robin Redfern/Ecoscene: 19tr.
Jochen Tack/Still Pictures: 18br. Thanks to our models, including Vanessa Dang, Sophie Hall, Latifah Harris,
Thomas Howe, Amelia Menicou, Spencer Mulchay, and Ishar Sehgal.

Contents

Smell and taste

Every day we smell and taste things in the world around us. Smelling and tasting are two of our senses.

▶ *We smell things with our nose.*

We have five senses. They are seeing, hearing, tasting, smelling, and touching.

◀ *We taste things with our tongue.*

5

Into the nose

Our nose takes in smells from the air. Smells float through the air.

▶ *We take in air when we breathe. We take in smells, too.*

Nostrils

6

The nearer we are to something, the better we can smell it.

We all have a nose on our face. Find a mirror and look at your nose. What shape is it? Can you see inside your nostrils?

This fox is sniffing the air to pick up smells.

7

Smells good!

Our noses take in many different smells. We like some smells.

Mmm! This food smells great!

These clothes smell fresh.

These roses smell sweet.

What smells do you like? Make a list of your five favorite smells.

9

Smells bad!

Sometimes our noses pick up nasty smells. We do not like these at all!

▶ *Ugh! These socks smell dirty.*

Pooh! The baby's diaper needs changing.

What smells don't you like? Make a list of the five smells you hate the most.

Yuck! This egg is rotten.

On the tongue

We taste our food when we put it on our tongue. We move the food around our mouth to taste it better.

▶ Different areas of our tongue pick up four different tastes.

Tastes bitter

Tastes sour

Tastes salty

When we chew, our teeth break up our food and make it taste stronger.

Tastes sweet

Working together

If food smells good, it will taste good, too! We need our sense of smell to taste our food.

► *If you hold your nose when you are eating, you cannot taste your food.*

Hold your nose and close your eyes. Ask a friend to pass you pieces of carrot and cucumber. Can you taste which is which?

When we try a new food, we smell it first…

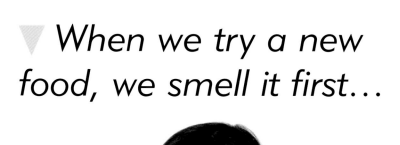

When we have a bad cold and our nose is blocked, we can't smell things well. What happens to our sense of taste?

then we taste a little.

15

How does it taste?

We don't all like the same tastes. We enjoy different kinds of food.

▶ *A good meal is made up of lots of different tastes.*

Some people love peanut butter.

Everyone has a favorite food. What's yours?

Some people hate it!

17

Keeping safe

Smells and tastes can protect us. They can warn us of danger.

▶ *The smell of smoke warns us of fire.*

▼ *We can smell when food is burning.*

A smell of gas warns us of danger.

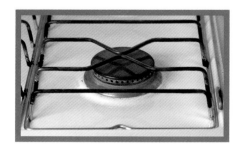

A vole sniffs the air as it feeds. It is smelling for hunters or other kinds of danger.

This milk tastes sour. It is not good to drink.

Take care of your body. Don't sniff or taste anything with a strong, nasty smell.

A world of tastes and smells

Our senses of taste and smell help to make life better. They help us to enjoy the world.

► *Without our senses, we could not taste lollipops…*

Smells and tastes help us remember things. What tastes and smells remind you of being on vacation?

and we could not smell the sea.

I know that...

1 We smell things with our nose.

2 We taste things with our tongue.

3 Smelling and tasting are two of our body's senses.

4 Our nose picks up many different smells—some good, some bad.

5 Our tongue picks up sweet, sour, salty, and bitter tastes.

6 We need to smell our food to taste it.

7 We enjoy different tastes.

8 Smelling and tasting help to protect us.

9 They help us to enjoy the world.

Index

About this book

I Know That! is designed to introduce children to the process of gathering information and using reference books, one of the key skills needed to begin more formal learning at school. For this reason, each book's structure reflects the information books children will use later in their learning career—with key information in the main text and additional facts and ideas in the captions. The panels give an opportunity for further activities, ideas, or discussions. The contents page and index are helpful reference guides.

The language is carefully chosen to be accessible to children just beginning to read. Illustrations support the text but also give information in their own right; active consideration and discussion of images is another key referencing skill. The main aim of the series is to build confidence—showing children how much they already know and giving them the ability to gather new information for themselves. With this in mind, the *I know that...* section at the end of the book is a simple way for children to revisit what they already know as well as what they have learned from reading the book.